OBJECTS AND FURNITURE DESIGN

# CHARLOTTE PERRIAND

© of the edition: 2020 Polígrafa
www.poligrafa.com

© of the images: Charlotte Perriand, VEGAP, Barcelona, 2017; Le Corbusier, FLC, VEGAP, Barcelona, 2017; Estate Pierre Jeanneret / ADAGP, Paris, 2017; Fernand Léger, VEGAP, Barcelona, 2017.

© of the texts, translations, and photographs: the authors

Researching and texts: Sandra Dachs, Patricia de Muga and Laura García Hintze

Design of the series: mot_studio

ISBN: 978-84-343-1494-8

Available in USA and Canada through D.A.P./Distributed Art Publishers
155 Sixth Avenue, 2nd Floor, New York, N.Y. 10013
Tel. (212) 627-1999 Fax: (212) 627-9484

Cover: Rocking chaise longue in bamboo and wood, 1940.

Backcover: Charlotte Perriand, ed., L'Art d'habiter, special edition, Techniques et architecture, no. 9-10, August 1950, p. 58.

Frontspiece: Proposition d'une synthèse des arts, Paris 1955, Le Corbusier, Fernand Léger, Charlotte Perriand exhibition, Tokyo, 1955.

OBJECTS AND FURNITURE DESIGN

# CHARLOTTE PERRIAND

Introduction by Josep Lluís Sert

Edited by Sandra Dachs, Patricia de Muga
and Laura García Hintze

Ediciones Polígrafa

# LIST OF CONTENTS

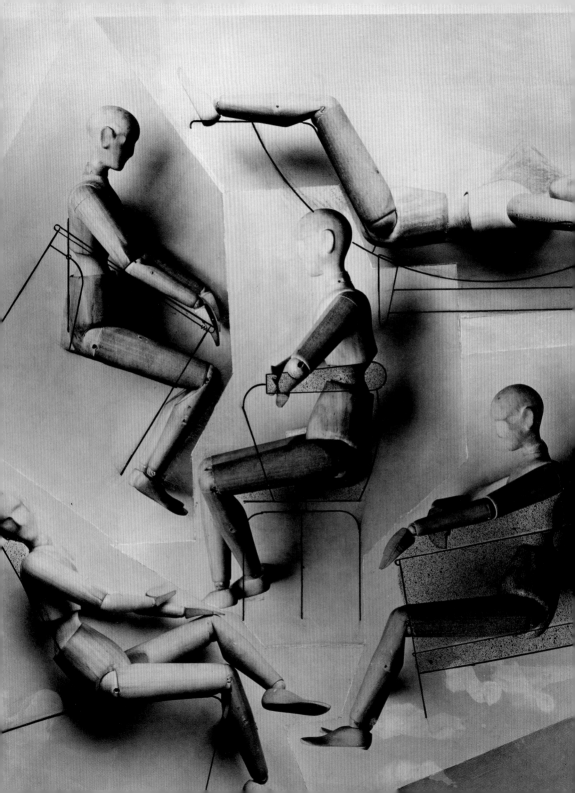

# INTRODUCTION

JOSEP LLUÍS SERT

First published as "Charlotte Perriand" in *L'Architecture d'Aujourdhui*, no. 7, March 1956, pp. 77-78

I had the pleasure and good fortune to meet Charlotte Perriand in Paris in 1929 at Le Corbusier and Pierre Jeanneret's studio on the rue de Sèvres. She belonged to the same international team of designers as I did, that, under Le Corbusier's aegis, witness new horizons opening up for architecture and urban planning and had memorable experiences in those fields. The CIAM [Congres Internationaux d'Architecture Moderne] had just been founded. There was still talk about the rejection, by an incompetent jury, of Le Corbusier and Pierre Jeanneret's design for the League of Nations headquarters in Geneva. A great war had come to an end only a few years before, [and] we dreamed of building a new world. The specter of the next war was still distant from us...

At the rue de Sèvres [studio], the concept of architecture also included urban planning and househould fittings, which are the natural extensions of architecture.

Charlotte Perriand fully grasped the new possibilities available to us all, possibilities of exploring unknown terrain. Our discussions on these subjects—urbanism, architecture, and household fittings—lasted from morning through night fall. We spoke of the discoveries and possibilities that industrialization would bring to our designs through the use of new materials. In terms of interior design pieces these new materials were, on the one hand, chromed tubular steel, folded sheet metal, and polished glass; on the other hand however, natural products such as waxed wood, cowhide, and others would also come into use as a reaction against this first tendency. I remember a bedspread by Charlotte that consisted of mosaic patchwork of stray cats's skins. . . on another instance I remember a carpet sent as a joke by Le Corbusier, Pierre Jeanneret, and Charlotte Perriand to an exhibition in Germany. The rug was composed of smaller rugs sold by traveling Turkish salesmen in cafes, [featuring] a yellow lion, an Eiffel Tower, a Queen of Spades, and other such images, all sewn together and obtained for an exorbitant sum of money. I don't know if the Germans, who have always taken architecture too seriously, appreciated this whimsical gesture. . . .

Charlotte arrived at the atelier each day with a new discovery—a photo or an object—which she would usually deem "adorable". It would be an unextravagant, simply contructed chair of beautiful proportions made of wood and rush, or a photo of the interior of a whitewashed, sparsely furnished, rustic country house with built-in cupboards, benches made of wood and rush, a table with wide planks and with all its wood's inconsistencies left plainly visible, and inexpensive color prints hanging on the walls.

Charlotte knew that expensive materials and refined design weren't everything. She soon went back to designing chairs with legs. The anonymous architecture of "the people" that she knew so well would lead her in a new direction. She was inspired by that "adorable" popular architecture that lacks a definitive style but that has remained prevalent throughout the centuries. This vernacular architecture challenges the concept of refinement; it is natural, human, and has its own kind of beauty that stems from its simplicity, continuity, and permanence. It doesn't quickly become out of fashion as other stylish objects do.

Charlotte loved vernacular architecture and rural items because she loved and understood people. During her mountain excursions, she lived with peasants and was surrounded by their things; she took on their qualities perfectly and was able to combine the best of rural furnishings with the best of what modern industry had to offer. As a result, Charlotte's furniture evokes a sense of harmony, tranquility, and timelessness that gives it a new and innovative edge. Her work has a continuity that stems from this sensitive and intelligent adaptation of everlasting forms to the needs of the given time.

It did not take long for Perriand to abandon chromed tubular steel and polished glass. She began to lose, little by little, her interest in luxury furniture pieces which were supposedly "mass-produced" and were made so that only a few privileged people could buy them. She discovered in the beginning that mass production required a larger market. Whenever her designs came in at a low cost, Charlotte was the happiest woman in the world. She was always most satisified upon solving problems concerning number increases.

The furniture of Charlotte Perriand is always splendidly structured; it is simple without being cold; its shapes, textures, and colors are balanced and harmonious. It is always carefully detailed, for Charlotte learned the lessons of fine craftsmanship and applied them to industrial production for she knew that these two things were combinable. She had a particular taste for aesthetic materials, that she savored as one would a good wine. She appreciated the diversity of textures and natural forms: large rocks from the Fontainebleau forest or shells and bits of wood gathered at the beach, which she managed to beautifully bring together, accompany her furniture pieces. In her home, beautiful photographs of mountains (as I suffered from the

Le Corbusier, Pierre Jeanneret, Charlotte Perriand, rocking chaise longue, 1928.

Parisian, chill, I'd have liked to see them disappear and even advised her to replace them with tropical landscapes) were displayed alongside paintings by Beauchamp [André Bauchant] and [Fernand] Léger and objects made by primitive peoples. This might seem like nothing special now, but twenty-five years ago. . . . Her taste for pure color brought her close to our dear friend Léger, who appreciated the similarity of her ideas to his own. He too, adored the colorful objects of the common people, the stalls at the fairs in the Paris suburbs and the city's bistros, the jukeboxes and taxis in New York, of which he always talked about. Charlotte worked with him on some photomontage projects for the International Exhbition in Paris in 1937. They shared a love for all that was simple and "of the people."

Thanks to their origins, the furniture designs of Charlotte Perriand retain an appeal that is almost always lacking in other designs from the same period. Furniture designs have a tendency to quickly become unfashionable, even more so than architecture. Few people could live today with the most sensational creations of twenty years ago. Chrome-plated tubes seem outdated now—they are more like museum pieces. . . they lack passion and their style is too distant from the human body. One doesn't sit on machines any more than one sits on paintings. . . .

Shortly before the outbreak of the Second World War Charlotte Perriand left for Japan where she remained until 1941. I saw Charlotte's first "Japanese" work in New York. Once again she had managed to discover what was best in popular traditions, a craftsmanship polished by the course of time much like a stone in a river, that harbored techniques that were at once simple and admirable. Using bam-

The Arc 1800 movable interior design, Les Mirantins, 1985-1987. Good use is made of the staircase space for storage.

Charlotte Perriand during her time in Japan between 1940 and 1942.

boo, she designed chairs that take advantage of the material's resilience and elasticity. These pieces were counterparts to [Alvar] Aalto's molded plywood furniture. She made good use of what was best in Japanese architecture, translating it into a modern language based on the intelligent regionalism that Japan's most gifted young architects had recently adopted. The taste for all things Japanese that had always lain dormant inside Charlotte was awakened by her trip to Tokyo, from which she returned with exhaustive documentations of Japanese architecture, furnishings, and everyday objects. Charlotte, who had always been interested in the links between architecture, household fittings, painting, and sculpture, organized an exhibition in Tokyo of her furniture along with paintings and tapestries by Léger and Le Corbusier. Judging from photographs, the resulting *ensemble* was

full of gaiety and life. It possessed, I'm sure, the special qualities of all of Charlotte Perriand's interiors—the moderation and balance that the French are famous for, and a vitality particular to her work alone.

Charlotte designed household furnishings as integral parts of the architecture of the residential unit, in the same way that the the residential unit itself is inseparable from the entire housing block, from the neighborhood, from the city itself— in other words, from everything belonging to our physical surroundings, to our habitat. The harmony of this habitat cannot be achieved independently from architecture and urban planning.

Upon establishing that the dwelling structure must function as an integral whole in its surroundings, Charlotte Perriand was able to understand the fundamental importance of empty spaces.

Bamboo chaise longue with rush cover made by Seccho, shown in Takashimaya, 1941.

Charlotte Perriand in 1928. Next to her, Le Corbusier holds a plate above her head in the manner of a halo.

She set out to design "furnishings that create emptiness" because space, in residential units, was becoming more and more precious. Hence she began to design her ingenious storage units, that could be perceived as screens or walls. "Without well-designed storage, emptiness in the dwelling is impossible. We opt for utilitarian walls." This same concept is valid on an even larger scale, in terms of architecture and urban planning, keeping in mind the importance of maintaining a human dimension. Everything that we encounter in our daily lives requires empty spaces in its surrounds— a majestic tree in a courtyard, a beautiful painting in a room, or a monument in a public square—all require emptiness. Charlotte Perriand creates interiors as an urban planner, distinguishing among a house's functions—food preparation, hygiene, housekeeping, storage, leisure, children's area, parents' area, etc. And upon doing this, she always transmits beautiful proportions, pure colors, and a vitality that is present in every aspect of her work.

Cambridge, Massachusetts, March 1956

# DRAWING ROOM CORNER

**Year:** 1926
**Location**
Salon of Interior
Design Artists, Paris

**Furniture**
WOOD AND LEATHER
ARMCHAIR (1) (2)
WOOD AND GLASS
CUPBOARD UNIT
WOOD AND GLASS TABLE

In 1926 Charlotte Perriand received her first commission, called Drawing Room Corner, to be shown at the exhibition organized by the Salon of Interior Design Artists. The intention was to create furnishings for the French middleclass that could be mass-produced, thereby demonstrating that modern decorative art was not reserved exclusively for a minority. Her design at this time was still imbued with the spirit of Art Deco, though this time without ornamentation and fantastical touches, as one can see in her wooden armchair. This chair introduces a number of subtle constructional innovations. The front legs are straight, whereas those at the back are curved to ensure that the seat, the volume of which has deliberately been reduced, remains firmly stable.

This armchair was ahead of its time in terms of its volume and was a forerunner of the line of swivel chairs yet to come.

(1)    (2)

Drawing Room Corner, Salon of Interior Design Artists, 1926.

# SWIVEL CHAIRS

**Year:** 1927-1930

›ARMCHAIR B 302
(1927) (1)
**Dimensions**
73 x 60 x 58 cm
**Edition**
1st.: Thonet, 1930
Contemporary: Cassina

›STOOL B 304 (1927) (2)
**Dimensions**
43 x 52 cm (diam.)
**Edition**
1st.: Thonet, 1930
Contemporary: Cassina

›OFFICE CHAIRS
FIRST MODEL
First version: 1927 (3)
Second version: 1928 (4)

›OFFICE CHAIR (1928) (5)

›TYPIST'S CHAIR B 303
(1930) (6)
**Edition**
1st.: Thonet, 1930

**Materials**
›Structure: chrome-plated
tubular steel
›Upholstery: feather
cushion (4) or
leather upholstery

**Colaboration (5) (6)**
Le Corbussier, Pierre
Jeanneret.

The wooden armchair made for the Drawing Room Corner exhibition was, in part, the forerunner of Perriand's swivel chairs (1, 2, 3 and 4). The swivel Chair B 302 (1) and the swivel Stool B 304 (2) designed by Charlotte Perriand were included in the Le Corbusier, Pierre Jeanneret, Charlotte Perriand range of furniture that Thonet began to issue in 1930. Contrary to legend, these two chairs were not designed by Le Corbusier. Only the Swivel Office Chair (5) and the Typist's Chair B 303 (6), both based on earlier chairs, are the result of the collaboration between Charlotte Perriand, Le Corbusier and Pierre Jeanneret.

(1)    (2)    (3)

(4)    (5)    (6)

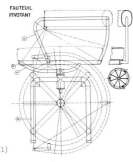

FAUTEUIL
PIVOTANT

(1)

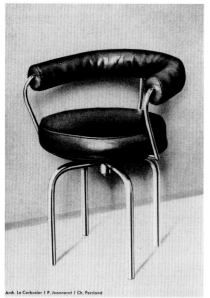

Arch. Le Corbusier / P. Jeanneret / Ch. Perriand

**B 302
Thonet**

(1)

(4)

Drawing of the functioning of the swivel chairs.

Perspective drawing of the design of the Salon of Interior Design Artists, 1928.

View of the Dining Room of 1928, with Perriand's tubular stools and a nickel-coated table from 1927. The glass wall calls to mind the facade of the architect's attic apartment in place Saint-Sulpice.

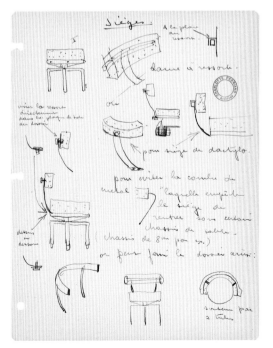

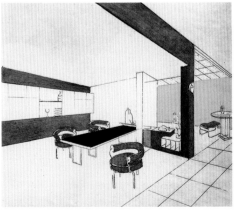

# BAR IN THE ATTIC

**Year:** 1927
**Location**
Salon d'Automne, Paris

**Furniture**
HIGH STOOL
LOW STOOL
COCKTAIL TABLE
CARD TABLE

In 1927, Charlotte Perriand and her husband moved to an attic apartment in Place Saint-Sulpice in Paris. It was there that she began to experiment with tubular steel structures. Her bar was designed for the apartment entrance and that same year was shown at the Salon d'Automne. It consisted of a bright room made up of a combination of nickel, aluminum, mirrors, and leather upholstery—a sophisticated blend of bohemian style and luxury chic, a space that was at once both domestic and urban where she could relax with her friends. The pieces that stand out the most are the square card table with four indentations for aperitif glasses and the low leather stool. They both have similar bases consisting of nickel-coated panels that cross at the center. Although Charlotte Perriand distanced herself from her conservative contemporaries with her fresh and youthful interior space innovations, the logic of the shapes she used was still determined by the ideals of Art Deco.

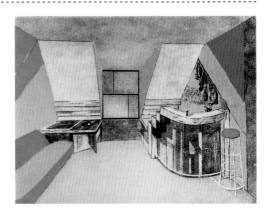

Perspective drawing of the Bar in the attic, Salon d'Automne, Paris, 1927.

Bar in the attic, Salon d'Automne, Paris, 1927.

LOW STOOL
**Year:** 1927
**Materials**
›Structure: nickel-coated
3-mm steel panels
arranged in a cross
›Seat: padded,
leather upholstery

COCKTAIL TABLE
**Year:** 1927
**Materials**
›Structure: nickel-coated
3-mm steel panels
arranged in a cross
›Top: round sheet glass

## CARD TABLE

**Years:** 1927 and 1928 (variant)

**Materials**

> Structure: nickel-coated
3-mm steel panels
arranged in a cross
> Top: square sheet glass
> Leaf variant: wood and
nickel-coated copper

**Variant**

Foldaway table
(1928)

# EXTENDABLE TABLE

**Year:** 1927
**Materials**
›Structure: chrome
tubular steel
›Top: slats of wood
covered with rubber with
chrome steel frame
›Plywood box lacquered
in white to conceal
the table top
**Dimensions**
72 x 180 (300 cm fully
extended) x 91 cm
**Edition**
1st.: Thonet, 1930 (Deluxe
edition)
Contemporary: Cassina

The starting point for the design of these tables consisted of a tubular frame onto which one or more boards could be placed as required. The first development of this design consisted of U-shaped iron sections that allowed the frame to be extendable in the same way that a telescope is.

In a later stage, Perriand attempted to create a table that could roll out, consisting of strips of wood on a very thin, moldable metal structure that could be stretched out. It was then that the term "extendable table" was first used.

Perriand made this table for her attic studio on Place Saint-Sulpice in 1927. In 1930, she designed a version with a lever system and castors that is known as the "Deluxe edition".

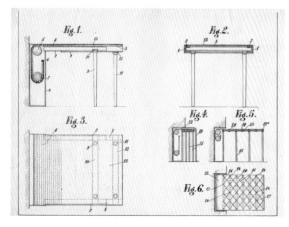

Drawing of the extendable table submitted as part of the patent application (previous page).

Reproduction of the dining room in Perriand's attic apartment on Place Saint-Sulpice, designed for the exhibition at the Salon of Interior Design Artists, Paris, 1928.

Deluxe Edition Extendable Table with castors and extending system with
lever, exhibited alongside metal furniture designed by Le Corbusier,
Jeanneret and Perriand at the first Exhibition of the Union of Modern
Artists, held in the Museum of Decorative Arts, Paris, 1930.

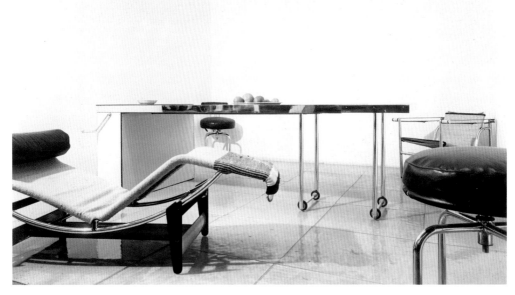

Drawing of the Deluxe Edition extendable table.

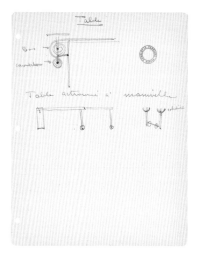

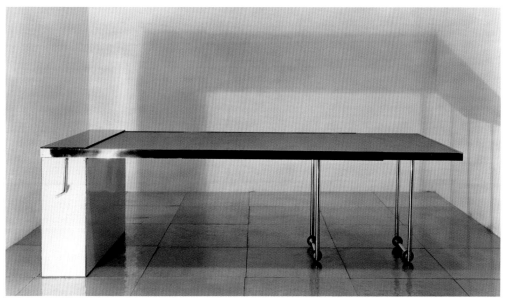

# GRAND CONFORT ARMCHAIR

**Year:** 1928
**Materials**
›Structure: tubular steel
›Seat, back and
armrests: 4 removable
leather cushions
**Dimensions**
67 x 97 x 70 cm
**Collaborators**
Le Corbusier and Pierre
Jeanneret
**Edition**
1st.: Heidi Weber,
1959-1964
Contemporary: Cassina

Around 1925 many designers were rein-terpreting the traditional English leather armchair, which represented the archetype of bourgeois comfort and was among Le Corbusier's *objets types*. These armchairs, together with the cubic chair that Perriand had designed for Travail et Sport, served as point of departure for the Grand Confort Armchair. The cubic chair consisted of a parallelepiped formed by a base surround-ed by a large U-shaped element. The Grand Confort Armchair has three large cushions that form the back and armrests which are arranged around the seat with a tubular structure wrapped around them. In a later version from around 1929, which was nev-er brought to continuation, the base of the rear legs introduced a system of modifica-tion of the angle of inclination of the seat, thereby accentuating the reclining position of the occupant. Perriand designed a num-ber of variants of this armchair—large and small models, a two-seater, *canapé* and *méridienne*—drawing up a system that would meet every possible need.

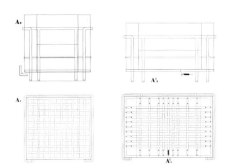

Elevation of the Grand Confort Armchair (pervious page).

Grand Confort Armchair, prototype, 1928.

Drawing of the various versions of the Grand
Confort Armchair.

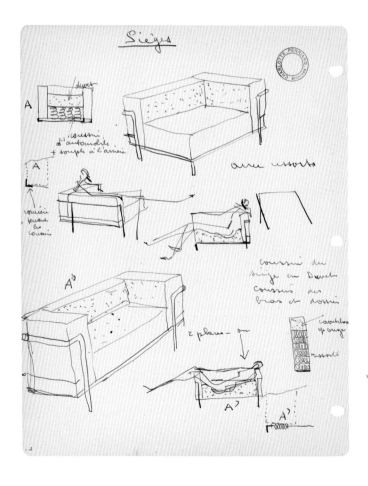

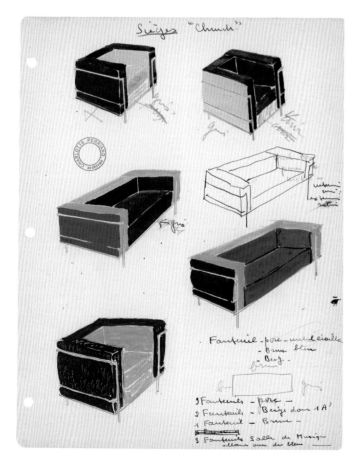

Sièges "Church"

Fauteuil - porc - métal eicaillé
- Brun bleu
- Beige.
brun.

3 Fauteuils - porc -
2 Fauteuils - Beige dont 1 A
1 Fauteuil - Brun -
3 Fauteuils Salle de Musique
villeum mm du bleu.

# ROCKING CHAISE LONGUE B 306

**Year:** 1928
**Materials**
› Structure: steel,
chrome finish
or varnished in opaque
black
› Seat: leather
upholstery
**Dimensions**
› Base: 54 x 158.8 cm
› Seat: 70 x 56.4 x 160 cm
**Collaborators**
Le Corbusier and Pierre
Jeanneret
**Variant**
Bamboo chaise longue
(1940)
**Edition**
1st.: Thonet, 1930
2nd.: Heidi Weber,
1959-1964
Contemporary: Cassina

It is difficult to pinpoint the authorship of each designer in the furniture pieces that Perriand worked on with Le Corbusier and Jeanneret. At first, Le Corbusier would establish the design parameters and suggest the basic form and Perriand would develop the form and add details, then Le Corbusier would check the final outcome. In her auto-biography, however, Perriand recounts that as Le Corbusier became impatient whenever he saw that she was not strictly following his drawings for the chaise longue to the let-ter, she took the liberty of creating the pro-totypes on her own in her apartment. After she completed the pieces, Perriand invited Le Corbusier and Jeanneret to see them; they were delighted with her work. From them on Perriand took on the responsibility of both the design and execution of the furniture pieces.
In 1940, Perriand created the chaise longue made of small strips of bamboo which, owing to their pliability, could comfortably support the curve of a human back. As in the original design, the angle of inclination of the chaise longue could be adjusted manually by sliding the body along the wooden base.

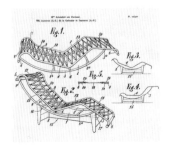

Drawing submitted with the patent application for the Chaise Longue in the names of Charlotte Perriand, Le Corbusier and Pierre Jeanneret, 1929 (previous page).

One of the precedents: Thonet's rocking chaise longue model no. 7500 (c. 1880).

Charlotte Perriand in the chaise longue, 1929

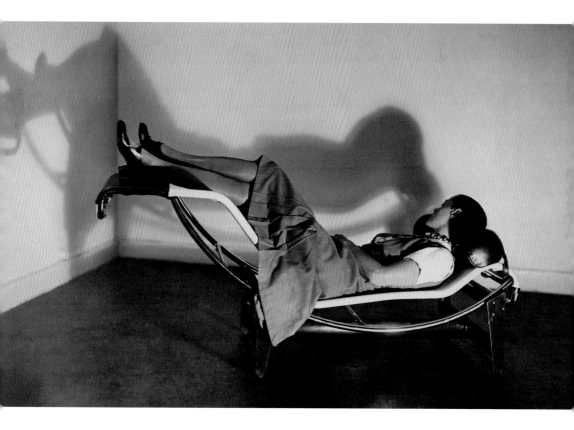

Study sketches of the chaise longue by
Charlotte Perriand, pastel on tracing
paper, 1928. (1)

Tubular steel chaise longue B 306. (2)

View of the gallery space at Villa La Roche,
Paris (Le Corbusier and Pierre Jeanneret,
1922-23) with the new furnishings
designed by Perriand, Le Corbusier and
Pierre Jeanneret in 1928. (3)

Next page: structure of the tubular
steel chaise longue B 306 (top) and the
structure and support of the bamboo
chaise longue (bottom). (4)

(1)

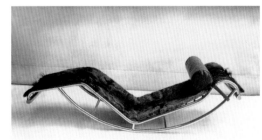

(2)

(3)

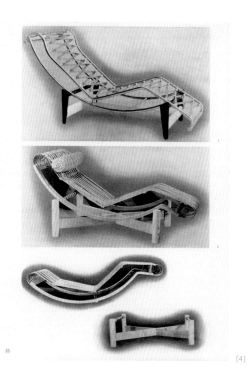

BAMBOO
CHAISE LONGUE (5)
**Year:** 1940
**Materials**
>Structure: wood
>Seat: bamboo strips
**Dimensions**
65 x 150 x 65.5 cm
**Edition**
1st.: Takashimaya, 1941
Contemporary: Cassina

33

(4)

(5)

# ARMCHAIR B 301

**Year:** 1928
**Materials**
> Structure: chrome tubular steel
> Seat and back: calfskin, wool, or canvas
> Armrests: leather strips
**Dimensions**
67.5 x 67 x 66 cm
**Collaborators**
Le Corbusier and Pierre Jeanneret
**Edition**
1st.: Thonet, 1930
2nd.: Heidi Weber, 1959-1964
Contemporary: Cassina

The original design for the Reclining Armchair B 301 was shown for the first time in the Salon d'Automne of 1929. Following the exhibition, the Thonet Frères company in Paris took on the project of developing it.

The original chair was made available in a number of different types of upholstery, initially with satin cushions and later with fabric or calfskin leather stretched tight and attached directly to the frame. The back of the chair was left open, allowing for the upholstery to be removed.

In 1930, Thonet introduced the closed back and then later, as a result of complaints from customers, made a small modification in 1932 by adding rubber stops to secure the tilt of the reclining back. (1) The final variant was issued under the name of "Exécution de Luxe" and was available with another type of cushion covering.

(1)

Detail of the tubular structure of the armchair B 301,
version with rubber stops for the back (previous page).

Side elevations of the armchair B 301.

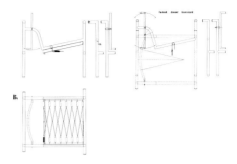

# APARTMENT FURNITURE

**Year:** 1929
**Location**
Displayed at the Salon
d'Automne
**Presentation**
Interior furnishings
for a room set up in a
100 m² stand
**Collaborators**
Le Corbusier and Pierre
Jeanneret

**Furniture**
COMPARTMENT
MODULES
STOOL B 305

In 1929, as part of the Salon d'Automne held each year in Paris, Le Corbusier, Jeanneret and Perriand presented their new furniture. They installed the two-month long furniture exhibit in a 100 m² standard apartment for two people. The main purpose was to demonstrate the functional and flexible nature of the displayed furnishings and their rearrangements in the various rooms in the apartment. For example, the modular compartmented storage furniture made up of standard, combinable units that could be assembled and dismantled, were used to separate the living areas from the rest of the apartment. The bathroom itself divided the two bedrooms in the apartment by means of a single metal cylindrical cubicle that served as the shower. A metal rod running along a shelf served both as a towel rail in the bathroom as the bed headboard.

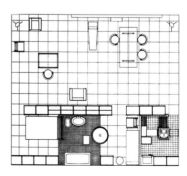

Floor plan of the apartment. Drawing by Arthur Rüegg
(previous page).

View looking from the drawing room to the dining room, 1929.

View of the master bedroom, followed by the bathroom with cylindrical shower in the middle and single bedroom in the background.

View of the master bedroom from the bathroom.

COMPARTMENT
MODULES
**Year:** 1929
**Materials**
›Structure: metal
modules (first model
made of bent sheet
metal with welded joints)
›Partitions and sliding
doors: mixed materials:
enameled metal,
glass or mirror surfaces

**Dimensions**
›Single-height module:
75 x 75 x 50 cm
›Double-height module:
150 x 75 x 50 cm
**Collaborators**
Le Corbusier and Pierre
Jeanneret

STOOL B 305
**Year:** 1929
**Materials**
›Structure: tubular metal
›Seat: soft fabric
(toweling),
interchangeable
**Dimensions**
45 x 50 x 40 cm
**Edition**
1st.: Thonet, 1930
Contemporary: Cassina

The first model, designed by Charlotte Perriand, had a structure made of nickel-coated copper and a wicker seat that could be disassembled.

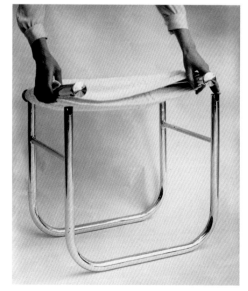

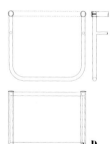

D₁

# DINING ROOM TABLE

**Year:** 1935
**Materials**
> Structure: wooden legs
> Board: solid wood
of 4 cm thickness

This piece, designed in 1935 for Paul and Ange Gutmann, was the first solid wood table built by Perriand. Its sturdy, broad top is reminiscent of the marble table that Perriand, Le Corbusier and Jeanneret designed for Le Corbusier's own apartment in 1934. This dining table is composed of the assembly of four grooved lengths of wood that are 6 cm wide and 2 cm deep surrounded and held in place by a perimetric piece also made of wood. The four legs are situated at farthest possible ends of the table, occupying an oblique position in relation to the center of the piece in order to ensure they present the smallest possible obstacle for diners' legs.

View of the dinning room in Étienne Sicard's Tokyo apartment, 1941.

# THE *MAISON DU JEUNE HOMME*

Year: 1935
**Location**
International Exhibition
in Brussels
**Collaborators**
René Herbst (gym
area), Louis
Sognot (rest and
sanitary areas),
Le Corbusier and
Jeanneret
(collaboration in
the furnishings)

**Furniture**
DESK
MANIFESTO SIDEBOARD
ARMCHAIR No. 21


DESK
**Year:** 1935 (based on
a 1934 model)
**Materials**
›Structure: cast
Corolle feet
›Board: slate
**Collaborators**
Le Corbusier and Pierre
Jeanneret
**Edition**
Contemporary: Cassina

Perriand worked on the design of the *Maison du Jeune Homme* with René Herbst and Louis Sognot, who had different creative sensibilities but shared the same concept of modernity. The project dealt with a theme that Perriand had already worked on in 1927: Work and Sport.

Perriand designed the interior of the study, in which every element is endowed with meaning: the slate wall on which the young man can write his thoughts, the wall of "objects [that stir up a] poetic reaction", the slate-topped table, the Manifesto Sideboard, etc. The *Maison du Jeune Homme* represents the essence of the modern spirit: the "synthesis of the arts" that serves everyone, that brings together in a single work interior architecture, painting, design, photography, and the sculpture found in nature.

Le Corbusier also used the Manifesto Sideboard as a support for propaganda: the central module was engraved with the Plan Voisin, while one of the side modules had a drawing on the glory of Paris.

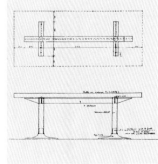

Parcial view of the *Maison du Jeune Home* at the International Exhibition in Brussels, 1935.

MANIFESTO SIDEBOARD
**Year:** 1935
**Materials**
>Structure: Corolle feet
>Three Standard
Flambo modules
finished in lacquered
sheet metal: one
contains a gramophone
and a radio receiver
**Collaborators**
Le Corbusier and Pierre
Jeanneret

## ARMCHAIR WITH FIXED BACK NO. 21

**Year:** 1935 (adaptation of Armchair B 301 from 1928)

**Materials**
> Structure: wood
> Seat and back: straw

**Dimensions**
72 x 65 x 55 cm
(Seat height: 40 cm)

**Edition**
1st.: L'Équipement de la Maison, 1947
2nd.: BCB, 1952
3rd.: Sentou, 1970

# FOLDING, STACKING CHAIR

**Year:** 1928-1936
**Materials**
> Structure: tubular steel
> Seat and back: fabric fixed to the structure
> Optional cushions: fabric or leather

The first sketch of these chairs dates from 1928, but they were not made until 1936 for the third Salon des arts ménagers exhibition, organized by *L'Architecture d'aujourd'hui*.

Perriand's most innovative idea in the displayed living room was her fusion of the functional workplace furniture with domestic furnishings. The folding, stacking chairs are a timeless design; they are made up of a piece of fabric attached to a tubular frame. The chair can be used as it is or with a padding consisting of two or three separate cushions stitched together. Folded one on top of each other, the cushions form a pouffe, and when extended out, a mattress. The numerous types of camping chairs that appeared after the war were directly inspired by Perriand's chair.

Drawing of the functionalities of the folding, stacking chairs.

Living room shown at the Salons des arts ménagers, 3º Exposition de l'habitation, organized by *L'Architecture d'aujourd'hui* magazine, 1936.

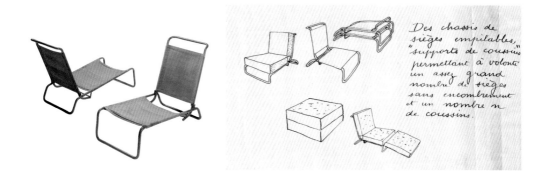

Des chassis de
sièges empilables,
"supports de coussins"
permettant à volonté
un assez grand
nombre de sièges
sans encombrement
et un nombre n
de coussins.

# LOW EASY CHAIR
# AND MÉANDRE SOFA

**Year:** 1937
**Materials**
› Structure: wood,
cross-braced system
› Cushions: canvas,
raffia or calfskin
**Variants**
Méandre sofa, 1937 (1)
Low easy chair with
cushions, 1937 (2)
Low bamboo easy chair,
1940 (3)
Bambou chair,
cross-braced system,
1940 (4)

After encountering many difficulties, the UAM (Union of Modern Artists) managed to build its pavilion at the 1937 World's Fair in Paris. The pavilion was one of the few French works that portrayed a truly modern spirit. In it, Perriand showed a series of affordable items of furniture made out of wood. These included her low easy chairs and Méandre sofa, a low table, and other furniture pieces on castors. With this easy chair and sofa design, Perriand developed a new type of structure known as the cross-braced system. In this design, the cushions are stitched together to form the seat and back of the chair and make the piece supremely comfortable. The legs of the low tables can be fitted into one of the legs of the chair or sofa, thereby allowing multiple combinations.

A few years later, during her stay in Japan, Perriand reworked a number of her models dating from 1936 to 1938, among them this easy chair and sofa. Due to the state of poverty in the country, she began to experiment solely with wood and bamboo.

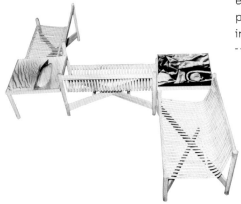

(1)

(1)

(2)

(3)

# HEXAGONAL TABLE

**Year:** 1938
**Materials**
> Structure: three circular wooden legs
> Top: six-sided polygon made of solid deal

In 1938, in order to make the best possible use of the space in her small studio on Boulevard Montparnasse, Perriand designed the first table of the series that would later become known as free-form furniture. Because the limited available space in her studio made it impossible for her to fit a round table for eight into her apartment, Perriand designed a polygonal table that was specifically tailored to her available space. She determined the dimensions of each side according to the number of people who were to sit facing each other. With this as a starting point, Charlotte Perriand moved away from using regular geometrical forms and instead introduced asymmetry as a symbol of freedom and protest against the established order of the time.

Sketch of the six-sided table from
the front and above.

Charlotte Perriand's apartment on
Boulevard Montparnasse, 1938.

# BOOMERANG DESK

Year: 1938
Materials
>Structure: three solid
wood legs
>Top: solid wood

This office desk was designed for Jean-Richard Bloch, the codirector along with Louis Aragon of *Ce soir* magazine. One of the key premises of the assignment was that the table had to be able to seat all ten members of his staff. Perriand after having studied Bloch's request and working habits along with some important ergonomic principles, designed the desk in the form of a boomerang. The shape of the table allowed the director, sitting on the inner side of the boomerang, to reach items anywhere on the table without hardly having to raise himself from his chair, and at the same time provided him with the option of various different working areas. The shape and size of the desk also provided space for ten people to sit around its outer edge. Once again, the application of asymmetrical forms helped her to better resolve space-intended use problems.

# GUÉRIDON TABLE No. 10

**Year:** 1938 (1)
**Materials**
›Structure: varnished wood
(ash or mahogany),
›Crosspieces:
ash and pine
›Top: wood or stone from
Hauteville.
**Edition**
1st.: L'Équipement de la
Maison, 1947
2nd.: BCB, 1952
**Variants**
›Coffee table with square top,
1940 (2)
›Doron Table, 1947-1948 (3)

In the late 1930s Perriand began to design a "rustic" series of furniture made in the main out of wood and in keeping with the "rural" and outdoor life that she herself loved so much.

One of the first pieces was the Guéridon table, which has a sturdy, triangular shape and which was intended for her apartment on Boulevard Montparnasse. During her time in Japan in the early forties Perriand designed several tops for the same table structure. She used local Japanese materials such as cane and bamboo. The Guéridon table also made later appearances in her interior designs for rural settings, such as the Méribel-les-Allues ski resort hotel (1946-48). Perriand used these designs as opportunities to continue experimenting with combinations of natural materials (wood, rush, hide, etc.) and to invent pieces with a warm, homely style that later became known as the "modern Savoy style".

(1)                    (2)                    (3)

Room in the Hotel Le Doron, Méribel-les-Allues, 1947-48.

# FOLDING CHAISE LONGUE

**Year:** 1939-1940
**Materials**
> Structure: wood with slats of the same material
> Padding made of three joined cushions

Perriand designed the Folding Chaise Longue in 1939 before her stay in Japan. She first began to explore this very economical type of chair back in 1926-1928. The unusual feature of this folding chaise longue is that it can be used not only as a chaise longue but also as a low armchair by folding the end underneath the seat and folding up the cushions, and as a day bed. Its small size allows it to be stored in a cupboard. In Japan, Perriand had several different cushions made of natural fibers or straw using traditional techniques. She showed the Folding Chaise Longue in the *Tradition, Creation, Selection* exhibition in Tokyo and Osaka in 1941. This kind of rest chair did not exist in Japan.

Drawing of the functioning of the folding chaise longue, 1928.

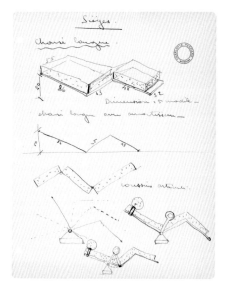

# SIDEBOARD

COMPARTAMENT
FOR SCAL FACTORY,
(ISSOIRE)
Year : 1939
Materials
> Structure: solid pine wood
> Sliding doors: aluminium

To meet the need for storage in the room, Perriand drew on an idea that Le Corbusier had theorized about in 1925 and developed the concept of the *casier* (compartment) that could be stacked, placed side by side, and combined. Following the commercial failure of the metal compartments shown at the Salon d'Automne in 1929, she designed compartments with a wooden structure and doors made of glass, aluminum, or wood. In 1936, she published the plans for these units and advice on how to make them in a popular magazine with a large circulation so that the public could have them made by craftsmen. Two years later, on the advice of Pierre Jeanneret, she revised the design by adding a new type of plywood sliding door with a long vertical handle, which she had profiled into an ergonomic shape so that the door can be easily opened and closed. Afterwards, many creators, among them Jean Prouvé, employed this principle for all their storage units with sliding doors.

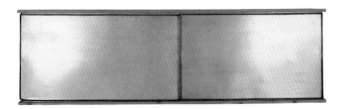

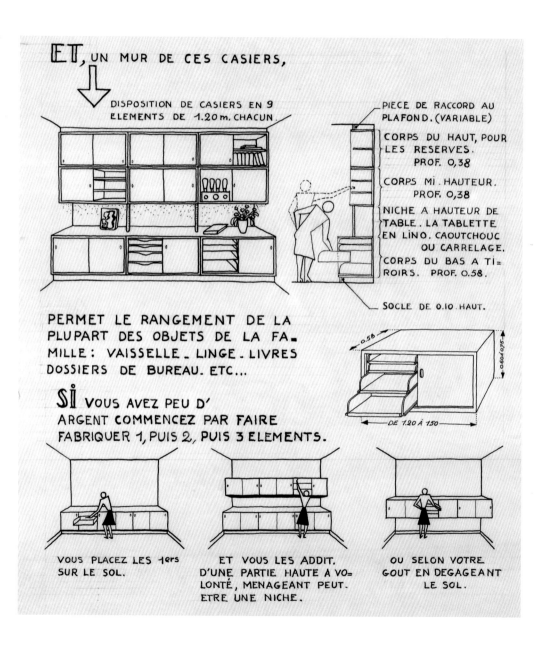

ET, UN MUR DE CES CASIERS,

DISPOSITION DE CASIERS EN 9
ELEMENTS DE 1.20 m. CHACUN

PIECE DE RACCORD AU
PLAFOND. (VARIABLE)

CORPS DU HAUT, POUR
LES RESERVES.
PROF. 0,38

CORPS MI . HAUTEUR.
PROF. 0,38

NICHE A HAUTEUR DE
TABLE. LA TABLETTE
EN LINO. CAOUTCHOUC
OU CARRELAGE.

CORPS DU BAS A TI=
ROIRS. PROF. 0.58.

SOCLE DE 0.10 . HAUT.

PERMET LE RANGEMENT DE LA
PLUPART DES OBJETS DE LA FA-
MILLE: VAISSELLE . LINGE . LIVRES
DOSSIERS DE BUREAU. ETC...

SI VOUS AVEZ PEU D'
ARGENT COMMENCEZ PAR FAIRE
FABRIQUER 1, PUIS 2, PUIS 3 ELEMENTS.

0.58

0.60 A 0.75

DE 1.20 A 150

VOUS PLACEZ LES 1ers
SUR LE SOL.

ET VOUS LES ADDIT.
D'UNE PARTIE HAUTE A VO-
LONTÉ, MENAGEANT PEUT.
ETRE UNE NICHE.

OU SELON VOTRE.
GOUT EN DEGAGEANT
LE SOL.

**SIDEBOARD WITH LEGS (1)**
**Year:** 1939-1945
**Materials**
›Structure: wood
(or steel, Prouvé
construction)
›Sliding doors:
plywood,
aluminum or Plexiglas
**Dimensions**
Sideboard: two/three
doors: 96/121 x
164/246 x 41 cm
**Collaborator**
Pierre Jeanneret
**Edition**
1st.: L'Équipement de la
Maison, 1947
2nd.: BCB, 1952

**WARDROBE (2)**
**Year:** 1945-1946
**Materials**
›Structure and handles:
ash wood
›Interior: poplar wood
›Base and compartments:
deal wood
›Doors: mahogany
**Dimensions**
159 x 164 x 58 cm
**Collaborator**
Pierre Jeanneret
**Edition**
1st.: L'Équipement de la
Maison, 1947
2nd.: BCB, 1952

**SIDEBOARD FOR PAUL
AND ANGE GUTMANN (3)**
**Year:** 1931
**Materials**
›Structure: walnut wood
›Legs: tubular steel
›Sliding doors: glass
**Dimensions**
115 x 168 x 35 cm

(1)

(2)

(3)

Catalog of L'Équipement de la Maison with furniture designed
by Pierre Jeanneret and/or Charlotte Perriand, 1947.

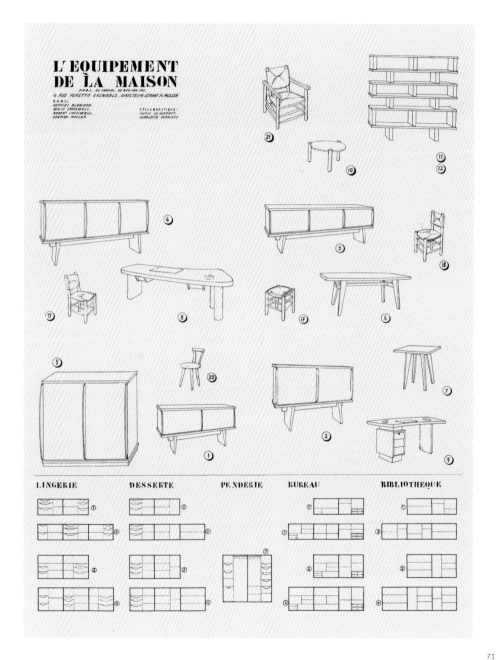

# DESK, TABLE AND SIDEBOARD STEPH SIMON EDITION

**FREE-FORM DESK (1)**
**Year:** 1939
**Materials**
> Structure and board:
Pine wood, three-plyboard
made of varnished
ash or oak
> Front drawer: aluminum
**Dimensions**
72 x 100 x 220 cm
Top: 6 cm thick
**Edition**
Steph Simon (from 1956)

**FREE-FORM TABLE (2)**
**Year:** 1959
**Edition**
1st.: Steph Simon, 1959
Contemporary: Cassina

**TABLE (3)**
**Year:** 1953
**Edition**
1st.: Steph Simon, 1956

In 1956, Steph Simon opened a gallery on Boulevard Saint-Germain in Paris, placing it under the wings of two great designers whose furnishings he had made: Charlotte Perriand and Jean Prouvé. For ten years, the Galerie Steph Simon was the flagship of design in France. Perriand entrusted to him a collection of furniture: the Tunisie and Mexique type libraries, tables and desks, storage units, chairs, stools, armchairs, etc., which became design icons in the 1950s.

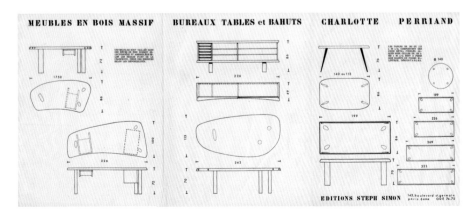

Catalog of solid wood furniture designed by Charlotte Perriand, produced by
Steph Simon, 1959 (previous page).

(1)

(2)

(3)

FREE-FORM
SIDEBOARD (4)
**Year:** 1939-1959
**Materials**
Various types of woods
**Edition**
1st.: Steph Simon, 1956
Contemporary : Cassina

SIDEBOARD (5)
**Year:** 1958
**Materials**
Various types of woods
and metal
**Edition**
1st.: Steph Simon, 1958
Contemporary: Cassina

STORAGE BLOC (6)
**Year:** 1958
**Materials**
Various types of woods
and metal
**Edition**
1st.: Steph Simon, 1958
Contemporary: Cassina

(4)

Charlotte Perriand Storage, produced by Steph Simon, 1958.

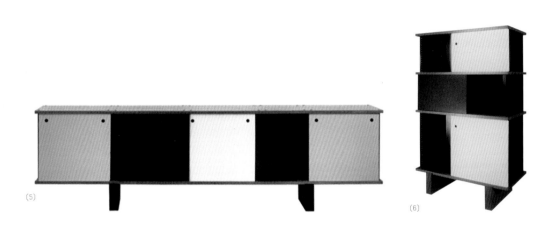

(5)

(6)

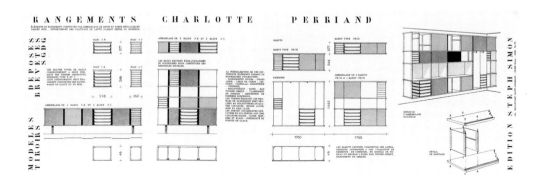

# MODULAR SOFAS
# AND SIDE TABLE

**Year:** 1940
**Materials**
>Structure: plywood
>Seat and back: bamboo
with fabric cushions
made by the Tatsumura
textile company (sofa)
>Table board: lacquered

In 1940 Perriand was invited to Japan by the Imperial Ministry of Trade and Industry in order to take on the position of adviser on industrial design. Her work consisted of steering Japanese productions toward the Western world. Her stay in the country was a learning experience in which she discovered much about Japanese traditions, became fascinated by the island nation, and absorbed many of its philosophies and customs. In 1941, she organized the *Tradition, Selection, Creation* exhibition at the Takashimaya department stores in Tokyo and Osaka. Perriand wanted to show how Japanese output could be adapted to suit Western ways. The modular sofas are a clear reflection of this intention, since this type of furniture is clearly Western, but in this case is developed using local techniques and materials.

*Tradition, Selection, Creation* exhibition at the Takashimaya department stores, Tokyo, 1941.

# BAMBOO ARMCHAIRS

**Year**: 1941
**Materials**
> Structure: plywood
> Seat and back:
a single piece
made out of
bamboo strips

In the aforementioned exhibition at the Takashimaya stores, two versions of Alvar Aalto's Cantilever Chair for Paimio Sanatorium (1931-32) were presented. These two armchairs feature curved strips of bamboo that, joined together, form the seat and back of the chair as a single piece. They are the outcome of Perriand's studies of and experimentation with the flexibility of bamboo. In Japan, Perriand came across a version of Alvar Aalto's Cantilever Chair done by a Japanese designer in bamboo (1). She was critical of this adapted design and produced her own solution in which the characteristics of bamboo as a material are exploited to the full (2).

Apart from these two chairs, the furniture Perriand showed in Tokyo and Osaka had been created in Paris well before her stay in Japan. She contented herself with adapting them to the Japanese manufacturing techniques employed at that time.

221. ALVAR AALTO, Armchair.

(1)

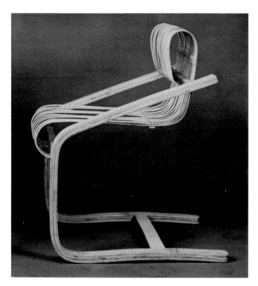

(2)

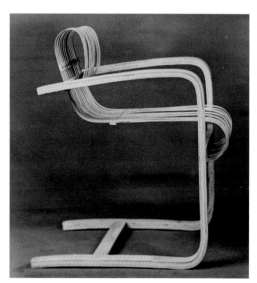

# FURNITURE FOR MÉRIBEL-LES-ALLUES

Year: 1947

CHAIR NO. 20 WITH
THREE LEGS (1)

CHAIR NO. 20 WITH FOUR
LEGS (2)

SWIVEL ARMCHAIR NO. 23
(1948) (3)

**Materials**
›Seat and back structure:
solid wood
**Edition**
1st.: L'Équipement de la
Maison, 1947 (1) (2)
2nd.: BCB, 1952 (1) (2) (3)

SQUARE TABLE NO. 7 (4).
**Edition**
1st.: L'Équipement de la
Maison, 1947
2nd.: BCB, 1952

One of Perriand's projects in the small town of Méribel-les-Allues, a new winter sports resort, was to fit out the interior space of an underground stable that had been converted into the Shangri-La nightclub. The wooden material used and the simple style of Perriand's furnishings for this assignment, including this three-legged chair, are the common denominators in the design of the space. The pieces that Perriand designed for this town throughout the forties once again reflect her desire to offer her vernacular architecture a fresh and open style that was also adapted to the specific needs of its location. These furnishings also demonstrate her desire to ensure that the spaces she designed were in keeping with modern times.

(1)  (2)  (3)

Shangri-La Nnightclub, Méribel-les-Allues, 1948.

(4)

# BERGER STOOLS

Year: 1947, 1953 and 1961

BERGER STOOL (1953) (1)
Dimensions
27 cm x 33 cm (diam.)
Edition
1st.: Steph Simon, 1956
Contemporary: Cassina

HIGH STOOL (1947) (2)
Edition
1st.: BCB, 1952

MÉRIBEL STOOL (1961) (3)
Dimensions
38.4 cm x 33 cm (diam.)
Edition
Contemporary: Cassina

Materials
›Structure and seat: oak wood

The Berger Stools, occasionally also known as Shepherd's Stools, were part of the furnishings that Perriand began to design for the hotel bar at the Méribel ski resort and which, toward the end of the forties, were added to the L'Équipement de la Maison catalogue. Her intention was to revive artisan-made furniture using cheap materials such as wood, while at the same time employing an expressive artistic idiom that could be adjusted to as affordable costs as possible. The postwar conditions in France at the time meant the country was clearly suffering from limited availability of materials and an absence of industrialists.

(1)          (2)          (3)

Bar at the Hotel Le Doron, Méribel-les-Allues, 1948.

# WARDROBES AND STORAGE UNITS

Year: 1949-1958

> COLLAPSIBLE
WARDROBE /
SHELVING MODULES,
(1949) (1)

> STORAGE UNITS,
(1954) (2)

> CUPBOARD FOR THE
MAISON DU SAHARA,
(1958) (3)

**Materials**
> Structure: wood or metal
> Drawers: bent aluminum
sheet, plastic or plywood

In 1946 Perriand returned to her study of storage and over a period of ten years she exhaustively analyzed the dimensions of everyday objects and went about perfecting the standardized elements of what she termed *"quincaillerie"* (hardware, ironmongery), such as drawers, cross-section structures, anchoring and bolt systems, runners, metal feet, etc. These played a fundamental role in her subsequent designs and enabled her to devise all sorts of furniture pieces.

In 1949, as part of the *Formes utiles, objets de notre temps* exhibition organized by the UAM in Paris, Perriand created a collapsible wardrobe with drawers made of sheet metal. One of the departments of the Aeronautical Construction Company studied the possibility of manufacturing this prototype industrially.

Another example of this kind of item of furniture is her system of stacking plastic drawers dating from 1954. In 1958, Perriand made a storage unit joined to a desk/bed headboard for the Maison du Sahara.

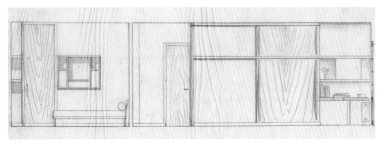

Study for storage for a hotel in Méribel-les-Allues, 1939.

Boîte transparente pour ac-
cessoires de pêche.
Boîte à couverts.
Matière plastique « Styron »
(Polystyrène). Dow Chemical
Cy U.S.A.

Aménagement intérieur de meubles ou de placards incorporés à l'architecture.
L'Unité est le tiroir coulissant, de forme conique, emboîtable, indéformable, fermé
ou non sur le devant ; il est en aluminium alumilité, édité par la S.C.A.N. ; il
peut être en plastique, en contreplaqué traité ; une étude économique en cours
définira le nombre et les matériaux appropriés.
Système breveté Ch. Perriand.

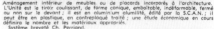

Boîte pour la conservation
des œufs dans le réfrigérateur.
Fichier Memo.
Boîte transparente pour ré-
frigérateur.
Matière plastique « Styron ».

(1)

Charlotte Perriand Storage equipment, produced by Steph Simon, 1956.

Storage units, 1954.

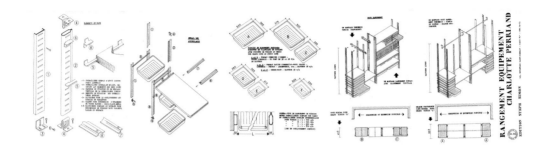

Drawing of the interior storage system and structure for stacking drawers, 1951.

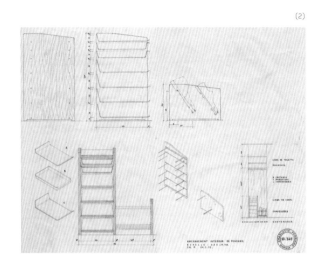

(2)

(2)       (3)

# LIBRARY TABLE FOR THE MAISON DE LA MÉDECINE

**Year:** 1951

**Materials**
> Structure: hollow triangular legs and lacquered steel crossbar
> Board: plywood
> Lamp: bent aluminum sheet

**Dimensions**
134 (74 + 60) x 420-303 x 113-115 cm

**Collaborators**
Jean Prouvé (production of the metal structure) and André Salomón (lighting consultant)

Perriand was commissioned to design the interiors of the Maison de l'étudiant at the Cité Universitaire in Paris. She designed this reading table, with lighting devises built into the structure itself, for the library. After ruling out more expensive models and proposals put forward by André Chetaille to be made out of wood, Perriand eventually decided to follow Prouvé's suggestion to make the table legs out of the cheapest option—bent steel. This piece is a clear example of Perriand's professional collaboration with Jean Prouvé's Ateliers in which she often applied the motto "beauty in utility" that she had learned at the school of the Central Union of Decorative Arts in Paris. This motto ended up becoming the hallmark of her working method.

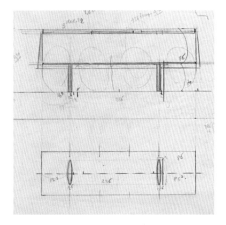

Library of the Maison de la Médecine (architects: Guy Lagneau and Michel Weill, interior design: Charlotte Perriand), 1950-1951 (previous page).

Various studies of the table lamp.

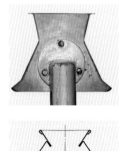

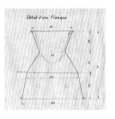

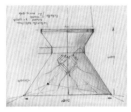

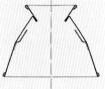

# LIBRARY UNITS

TUNISIE LIBRARY
UNITS (1)
**Year:** 1952
**Materials**
›Structure: lacquered
bent steel U-shaped
supports
›Shelves: deal wood
One piece U-shaped
supports know as "plot"
**Dimensions**
Height U-shaped
support: 13 cm, 21 cm
and 27 cm
**Edition**
Ateliers Jean Prouvé
(44 copies)

**Precursor**
Library Unit No. 11
(1940-1945) (2)
**Collaborator**
Pierre Jeanneret
**Edition**
1st.: L'Équipement de la
Maison, 1947
2nd.: BCB, 1952

(2)

In 1952 Charlotte Perriand signed a collaboration agreement with the Jean Prouvé studios whereby she undertook to aesthetically improve Prouvé's original furniture, to provide new designs suitable for mass production and to direct the creative work of the furnishings department of the studios founded by Prouvé.

As a part of this agreement, in 1952 Perriand designed a new type of library unit made of wood and metal, to be installed in 44 bedrooms in the Maison de la Tunisie students' residence in the Cité Universitaire in Paris. Shortly afterwards, Perriand created a new kind of shelving unit that met different requirements and served other functions, since books and objects arranged on it were accessible from both sides and it could be placed in the middle of a room. The design was gradually improved and was the key to the creation of a system based on combinable modules that could offer a wide range of different arrangements. The Tunisie and Mexique library became one of the most iconic pieces of furniture designed by Charlotte Perriand.

Drawings of the first studies for the Tunisie and Mexique libraries, 1952.

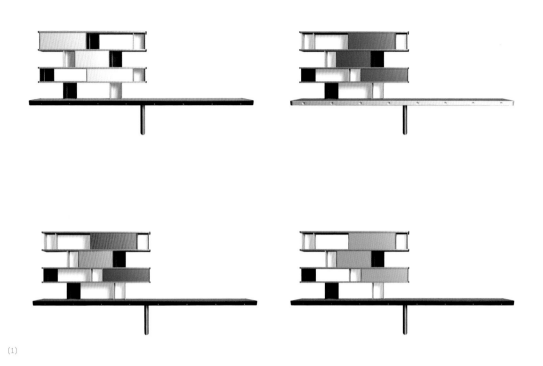

(1)

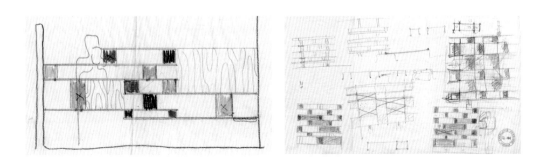

MEXIQUE LIBRARY
UNIT (3)
**Year:** 1952
**Materials**
>Structure: loadbearing
U-shaped
supports know as
"joues" in three parts.
Bent sheet lacquered
steel or aluminum
>Shelves: deal wood
**Dimensions**
U-shaped support:
13-21-27 x 21
x 14.3-15.3-24 cm
**Edition**
Ateliers Jean Prouvé
(77 copies)

›Charlotte Perriand
Library and Storage
Unit, Mexique type, (1st.
edition: Steph Simon,
1956; Contemporary:
Cassina)
›Charlotte Perriand
Library and Storage
Unit, Tunisie type,
produced by Steph
Simon from 1956.
›Nuage library, shown
at the Galerie Steph
Simon, 1956.

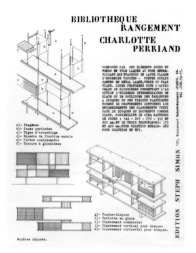

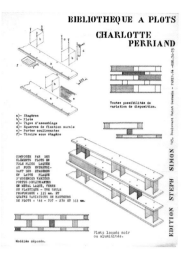

# TABLES WITH TRIANGULAR LEGS

**Year:** 1952-1956
**Materials**
›Structure: folded sheet metal legs
›Top: solid mahogany wood

›COFFEE TABLES
**Edition**
1st.: Steph Simon, 1956

›FULL-HEIGHT MODELS
**Edition**
1st.: Ateliers Jean Prouvé, 1955

The first table with this kind of structure was also known as the "mobile table" and was made for the cafeteria of the Maison de la Tunisie in 1952 (1). It was triangular in shape and had only three tall legs that were screwed to the wooden table top. This system of connecting the supports to the top enabled Perriand to design many variants simply by altering the shape of the table board. Thereafter Prouvé frequently used triangular-section legs in his furniture pieces.

(1)

Free-form coffee table on rug. *Proposition d'une synthèse des arts, Paris 1955.*
*Le Corbusier, Fernand Léger, Charlotte Perriand* exhibition, Tokyo, 1955.

Drawing of the table for the students' rooms in the Maison du Mexique, 1952.

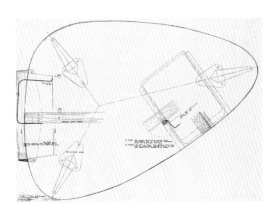

Drawing of the four versions of the table with triangular legs, 1953.

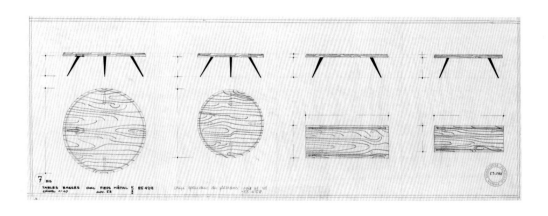

# LIGHTWEIGHT TABLES

**Year:** ca. 1947
**Materials**
›Structure: black
lacquered
tubular steel
›Top: varnished,
satin-finished, in black
or white oak or matte
plastic coating
**Collaborator**
Pierre Jeanneret
(first version ca. 1947)
**Edition**
1st.: Ateliers Jean
Prouvé (high table),
1953
1st.: Steph Simon (low
table), 1956

The first sketches of these tables were drawn circa 1947 by Pierre Jeanneret and Charlotte Perriand (1). The design was put into production about five years later as part of the furnishings in the rooms in the Maison de la Tunisie students' residence hall (2). The trapezoid shape table was intended to take up the least space possible and was lightweight to make it easier to move around the room. The table board was made of plywood with rounded edges and was less thick than that of previous tables, while the frame was tubular and therefore hollow. What's more, this table was one of the first to be sold under a revolutionary concept in the market at that time whereby professionals in the design and furniture sector were able to buy furniture parts separately in order to combine different colors and sizes.

(1)

(2)

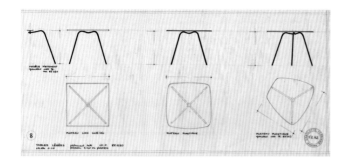

Drawing (detail) of the three versions of lightweight tables, 1953.

One of the students' rooms in the Maison de la Tunisie, 1952.

# BATHROOM FITTINGS

**Year:** 1937-1958

>DELAFON BATHROOM
(1937) (1)
**Collaborators**
Le Corbusier and Pierre
Jeanneret

>WALL-MOUNTED
TOILET (1951) (2)
**Collaborator**
Jean Borot

>WATER UNIT
(1957-1958) (3)


**Materials**
Ceramic

At the 1929 Salon d'Automne, Le Corbusier, Jeanneret and Perriand presented fixtures and fittings for a bedroom and connecting bathroom. Perriand insisted on the importance of hygiene for "modern man" and in 1937 developed a prototype independent bathroom cell that could be produced industrially and that was intended for hotels (1). The design of the toilet fitting allowed it to be used as a toilet, bidet and urinal all in one. The floor was made of separated wooden slats with gaps between them allowing the room to serve as a shower cubicle as well. In 1951 Perriand and her friend Jean Borot, who worked in the bathroom fittings industry, designed a wall-mounted toilet (2) that is regarded as crucial to the development of bathrooms. In 1957-1958 she designed the Water Unit (3), a compact unit that incorporated every bathroom fitting in one single piece and was intended for the restroom at the Maison du Sahara.

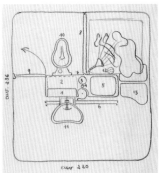

Study for of a bathroom published in "L'art d'habiter", special issue of *Techniques et Architecture* magazine no. 9-10, August 1950.

Drawing shown in the *Formes utiles* exhibition at the Salon des arts ménagers, 1952.

Plan and cross section of the Delafon Bathroom, 1937. Reconstruction by Arthur Rüegg and Barbara Thomenn. Drawing by Barbara Thomenn, 1998.

Prototype of the Delafon Bathroom displayed in the UAM pavilion at the 1937 World's Fair in Paris.

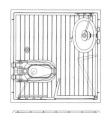

(1)

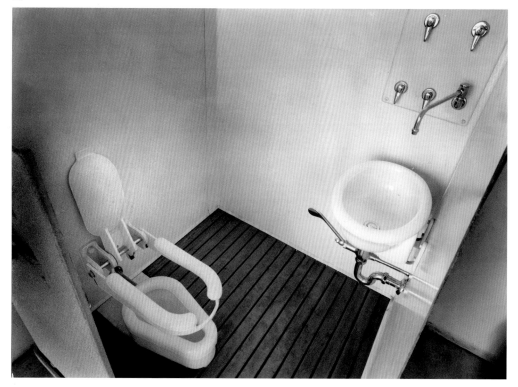

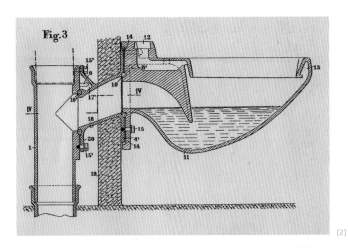

(2)

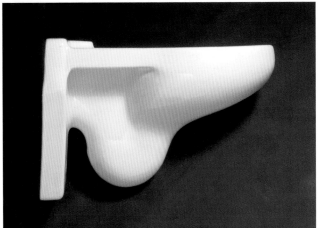

(2)

Study of sanitary fittings. Drawing by Charlotte Perriand and Pierre Jeanneret published in *L'Architecture d'aujourd'hui*, no. 11, May-June 1947.

Sketch of the rest cell of the Maison du Sahara in which the room and the Water Unit are separated by the storage space.

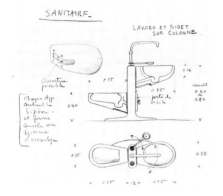

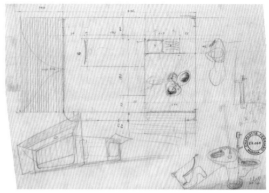

(3)

# OMBRE FURNITURE

**Year:** 1954

OMBRE CHAIR
**Dimensions**
64 x 50 x 51 cm
**Edition**
1st.: Tendo, 1954
Contemporary: Cassina

OMBRE EASY CHAIR
**Edition**
1st.: Tendo, 1954

**Materials**
› Structure: black
bent plywood
(later also available in
chrome-finish
or black varnished steel)
› Optional fabric
cushions

These chair and easy chair models were designed in Japan and shown at the *Proposition d'une synthèse des arts, Paris 1955, Le Corbusier, Fernand Léger, Charlotte Perriand* exhibition at the Takashimaya department store in Tokyo in 1955. They were inspired by Perriand's experiences and understanding of Japanese customs. One such custom was the puppet show known as Bunraku, in which the puppeteers dress and hood themselves and hence are able to operate the puppets while remaining abstract, barely visible forms. These shadowy figures are what inspired Perriand to name these particular fittings "shadow furniture" (*ombre* in French), and Perriand used these qualities to design the stacking black chairs so that they take on the quality of a "cloud hanging in the air around a long table".

View of the *Proposition d'une synthèse des arts, Paris 1955, Le Corbusier, Fernand Léger, Charlotte Perriand*, exhibition, Tokyo, 1955.

Views of the exhibition *Proposition d'une synthèse des arts, Paris 1955, Le Corbusier, Fernand Léger, Charlotte Perriand,* (Tokyo, 1955) with the Air France table and Ombre chairs and easy chairs (next page).

Ombre chair, 1954.

# STACKING GUÉRIDON TABLE

**Year:** 1953
**Materials**
A single sheet of
aluminum cut, molded
and anodized
**Edition**
Ateliers Jean Prouvé
(9 copies)

Stacking furniture is a feature of the Japanese tradition due to the need to store furniture away so as to leave spaces as uncluttered and open as possible. The stacking Guéridon Table is one of the items of furniture designed by Perriand for her husband in Tokyo, where he worked for Air France. The design is a reinterpretation of the food trays that were supported on black lacquered wooden legs and which were stacked away after use. Perriand adapted this idea to Western habits and created an individual table from a single piece of anodized black aluminum.

Design of the Air France stacking Guéridon table submitted to SPADEM (intellectual property rights board) in 1953.

# INFORMAL RECLINING CHAIRS

**Year:** 1954
**Materials**
> Structure: wood
> Optional padded
cushion and pillows
**Variants**
Informal reclining chairs
for one (1) or two
people (2)

These wooden reclining chairs, were presented at the second exhibition organized by Perriand in Japan, which she entitled *Proposition d'une synthèse des arts, Paris 1955, Le Corbusier, Fernand Léger, Charlotte Perriand*, and which was held at the Takashimaya department store in Tokyo. The country was recovering from the war at the time and Perriand, after two years of hard work, during which she was subjected to coercion on a number of occasions, managed to adapt the program of the exhibition to the limited financial resources available. In spite of the unpromising circumstances, she presented at the exhibition these recliners with a casual look that encouraged people to relax, converse and enjoy the company of others. These low seats are designed in accordance with Japanese customs, though they call to mind the chaise longue. During this difficult period, the artist's novel furniture was regarded as a luxury.

Informal wooden seat shown in *Proposition d'une synthèse des arts, Paris 1955, Le Corbusier, Fernand Léger, Charlotte Perriand*, Tokyo, 1955 (previous page).

Next page: View of the *Proposition d'une synthèse des arts, Paris 1955, Le Corbusier, Fernand Léger, Charlotte Perriand*, exhibition, Tokyo, 1955.

(2)

(1)

# TOKYO BENCH

**Year:** 1954
**Materials**
> Structure: solid oak wood
> Seat: 19 strips of oak wood
**Dimensions**
27 x 233 x 76 cm
(option with three legs shown, there were other variables)
**Edition**
1st.: Steph Simon, 1956
Contemporary: Cassina

The Tokyo Bench is a modular item of furniture that can serve a number of different purposes since it can function as a coffee table, as a bench, or even as a sofa with the addition of some cushions. Its geometry is very precise, in part due to the skilled artisanal assembly of the pieces of wood used to make it. The bench was presented at the *Proposition d'une synthèse des arts, Paris 1955, Le Corbusier, Fernand Léger, Charlotte Perriand*, exhibition at the Takashimaya department store in Tokyo in 1955 and exemplifies the new minimalist synthesis that Perriand incorporated into her work in wood during this period.

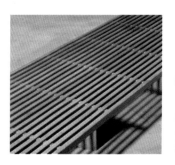

View of the *Proposition d'une synthèse des arts, Paris 1955, Le Corbusier, Fernand Léger, Charlotte Perriand* exhibition, Tokyo, 1955.

# CHRONOLOGY

CUPBOARD UNIT
1926
p. 19

WOOD AND LEATHER
ARMCHAIR No. 1 1926
pp. 18-19

SILVER CABINET
1926

HIGH STOOL
1927
pp. 24-25

LOW STOOL
1927
pp. 25-26

CARD TABLE
1927
p. 27

COCKTAIL TABLE
1927
p. 26

ARMCHAIR B 302
1927
pp. 20-21

STOOL B 304
1927
pp. 20-23

EXTENDABLE TABLE
1927
p. 29

SWIVEL OFFICE
CHAIR 1928
p. 20

GRAND CONFORT
ARMCHAIR 1928
pp. 32-35

CHAISE LONGUE
B 306 1928
pp. 36-38

ARMCHAIR B 301
1928
pp. 40-41

AIRPLANE TUBE TABLE
1928

STOOL B 305
1929
p. 47

TUBULAR STEEL BED
1929

COMPARTAMENT
MODULES 1929
p. 46

SWIVEL TYPIST'S
CHAIR B 303
1930   p. 20

LA SEMAINE À PARIS DESK
1930
p. 43

EXTENDABLE TABLE WITH CASTORS
1930
pp. 30-31

MARTEL LIBRARY
1930

RIVER ARMCHAIR,
FOR PLACING SIDE
BY SIDE 1930

SALVATION ARMY
BED
1933

MARBLE TABLE
1933

DINING ROOM TABLE
1934-1935
pp. 48-49

MANIFESTO SIDEBOARD
1935
p. 52

ARMCHAIR WITH
FIXED BACK No. 21
1935   p. 53

FOLDING, STACKING   LOW EASY CHAIR
CHAIR 1936          1937
pp. 54-55           p. 58

MÉANDRE SOFA
1937
pp. 56-57

FILING CABINET ON
WHEELS 1937
p. 58

DELAFON BATHROOM
1937
p. 101

TABLE WITH SLATE TOP
1937

MANIFESTE COFFEE
TABLE
1937

BOOMERANG DESK
1937
pp. 62-63

TABLES WITH
INTERCHANGEABLE
TOP 1937-1940

GUÉRIDON TABLE
No. 10 1937
pp. 64-65

WOODEN ARMCHAIR
1938

HEXAGONAL TABLE
1938
pp. 60-61

DINING TABLE
1938

DESK No. 8
1938
pp. 72-73

WALL CUPBOARD
1938

COMPARTMENT
1939
p. 68

TABLE No. 6
1939

FOLDING CHAISE LONGUE
1939-1940
pp. 66-67

LIBRARY UNIT
No. 11 1940-1945
p. 90

BAMBOO EASY CHAIR
1940
p. 58

BAMBOO CHAIR
1940
p. 59

MODULAR SOFAS
1940
p. 76

SIDE TABLE
1940
p. 76

TRONC BRUT COFFEE TABLE
1940

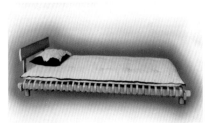

BAMBOO CHAISE LONGUE
1941
p. 39

BAMBOO BED
1941

BAMBOO ARMCHAIR
1941
pp. 78-79

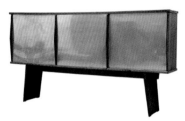

LIBRARY
1941

WOOD AND RUSH
CHAIR
1941

MARBLE TABLE
1941

SIDEBOARD WITH LEGS
1945-1946
p. 70

WARDROBE
1945-1946
p. 70

BOOMERANG DESK
1947

SQUARE TABLE
No. 7 1947
p. 81

DORON TRIANGULAR
TABLE
1947   p. 64

CHAIR No. 20
1947
pp. 80-81

WOOD AND CALFSKIN
EASY CHAIR
1947

BERGER STOOL
1947
pp. 82-83

TRIANGULAR TABLE,
HÔTEL DU DORON
1947

SWIVEL ARMCHAIR
No. 23 1948
p. 80

DISASSEMBLABLE
WARDROBE 1949
p. 85

KITCHEN BAR
1949

KITCHEN
1950

NEST TABLES
1951

WALL-MOUNTED
TOILET 1951
p. 102

LIBRARY TABLE
1951
pp. 88-89

BRAZZA CUPBOARD
1952

BRAZZA TABLE
1952

THREE-LEGGED
STOOL
1952

TABLE WITH TRIANGULAR LEGS
1952
p. 94

TABLE FOR THE
MAISON DE LA TUNISIE
1952  pp. 98-99

MAISON DU
MEXIQUE LIBRARY
UNIT 1952   p. 92

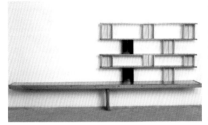

MAISON DE LA TUNISIE LIBRARY
1952
pp. 90-91

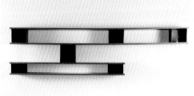

NUAGE LIBRARY
1953-1962

TELEPHONE TABLE
1953

STACKING TABLE
1953
pp. 108-109

OMBRE CHAIR
1954
pp. 106-107

OMBRE EASY CHAIR
1954
p. 105

INFORMAL
RECLINING CHAIR
1954   p. 111

INFORMAL
RECLINING CHAIR
1954   pp. 110-113

TOKYO BENCH
1954
pp. 114-115

STORAGE UNITS
1954
p. 87

SCREEN UNIT
1954

DINING TABLE
1954
p. 73

FREE-FORM COFFEE
TABLE
1954  p. 95

STORAGE WARDROBE
1954
p. 86

RECTANGULAR
TABLE 1954
p. 96

DESK
C. 1955

TABLE WITH
TRIANGULAR LEGS
1956  p. 97

LIBRARY-CUM-SCREEN,
AIR FRANCE, (LONDON)
1957

BOOMERANG BENCH, AIR FRANCE, (PARIS)
1957

WATER UNIT
1957-1958
p. 103

FREE-FORM
SIDEBOARD
1958  p. 74

STORAGE BLOC
1958
p. 75

PARTITION UNIT,
MAISON DU BRÉSIL
1958

ACCESSORY
STORAGE UNIT
1958

CUPBOARD FOR
MAISON DU SAHARA
1958  p. 87

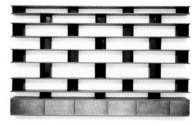

LIBRARY
C. 1958

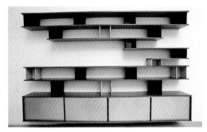

LIBRARY
C. 1958

SIDEBOARD
1958
p. 75

FREE-FORM
COFFEE TABLE
C. 1959

LIBRARY
C. 1960

LIBRARY
C. 1960

WALL LIGHTS WITH
PIVOTING SHADES
1962

RIO BENCH
1962

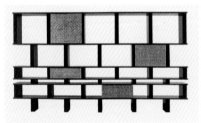

RIO LIBRARY
1962

CANE COFFEE TABLE,
JAPANESE EMBASSY,
PARIS 1968

BENCH, JAPANESE EMBASSY, PARIS
1968

HEIGHT-ADJUSTABLE
ENAMELED TABLE,
LES ARCS
1971

FAN TABLE
1972

PREFABRICATED
POLYESTER
BATHROOM, ARCS EN
SAVOIRE 1975

# BIBLIOGRAPHY

Laure Adler. *Charlotte Perriand*. Paris, Gallimard, 2019.

Jacques Barsac. *Charlotte Perriand. Un art d'habiter, 1903-1959*, Paris, Norma, 2005.

Jacques Barsac. *Charlotte Perriand et le Japon*, Paris, Norma, 2008.

Jacques Barsac. *Charlotte Perriand et la photographie. L'œil en éventail*, Paris, 5 Continents Editions, 2010.

Jacques Barsac, Sébastien Cherruet. *Le monde nouveau de Charlotte Perriand*. Paris, Gallimard, 2019.

Charlotte Benton. *Charlotte Perriand. Modernist Pioneer*, London, Design Museum, 1997.

*Charlotte Perriand*, Paris, Éditions du Centre Pompidou, 2005.

*Charlotte Perriand. L'aventure japonaise*. Milan: Silvana, 2013.

*Charlotte Perriand. Un art de vivre*, Paris, Flammarion y Musée des arts décoratifs, 1985.

*Charlotte Perriand. Une vie de création*, Paris, Odile Jacob, 1998.

*Charlotte Perriand, Fernand Léger. Une connivence*, Paris, Réunion des musées nationaux, 1999.

Olivier Cinqualbre et al. *UAM, Une aventure moderne*. Paris: Éditions du Centre Pompidou, 2018.

Ana Domínguez Siemens. "Charlotte Perriand. La pionera del interiorismo moderno", in *Diseño Interior*, no. 146, 2004, pp. 110-117.

Carmen Espegel. *Heroínas del espacio. Mujeres arquitectos en el Movimiento Moderno*, Valencia, Ediciones Generales de la Construcción, 2006.

Charlotte & Clementine Fiell. *Women in design: from Aino Aalto to Eva Zeisel*. London: Laurence King Publishing Ltd, 2019.

François Laffanour (ed.). *Living with Charlotte Perriand*. Paris: Skira, 2019.

*Le Corbusier, Charlotte Perriand, Pierre Jeanneret, "La machine à s'asseoir"*, Rome, De Luca, 1976.

"Le Corbusier. L'atelier 35 rue de Sèvres," in *Bulletin d'Informations Architecturales*, Paris, Institut français d'architecture, 1987.

*Massilia 2008. Encuentro de Granada*, Granada, Massilia, 2007.

Justin McGuirk (ed.), Octavio Camargo, Glenn Adamson, et al. *Charlotte Perriand: The Modern Life*. London: The Design Museum, 2021.

Mary McLeod (ed.). *Charlotte Perriand. An Art of Living*, New York, Harry N. Abrams y Architectural League of New York, 2003.

Mary McLeod. "Charlotte Perriand. Her First Decade as a Designer," in *AA Files*, no. 15, 1987, pp. 3-13.

María Melgarejo Belenguer. *La arquitectura desde el interior*, 1925-1937. Lilly Reich y Charlotte Perriand. Barcelona: Fundación Caja de Arquitectos, 2012.

*Modern Design for Living. Perriand, Jeanneret, Le Corbusier, Prouvé*, Paris, Artcurial, 2008.

Pernette Perriand-Barsac. *Charlotte Perriand, Carnet de montagne*, Chambéry, Maison des jeux olympiques, 2013.

Arthur Rüegg (ed.). *Charlotte Perriand. Livre de bord, 1928-1933*, Basel, Birkhäuser, 2004.

José Luis Sert. "Charlotte Perriand" in *L'Architecture d'Aujourd'hui*, no. 7, march 1956, pp. 77-78.

Elisabeth Védrenne. *Charlotte Perriand*, New York, Assouline, 2005.